# Ten Poems about Daughters

Candlestick Press

Published by:
Candlestick Press,
Diversity House, 72 Nottingham Road, Arnold, Nottingham NG5 6LF
www.candlestickpress.co.uk

Design and typesetting by Craig Twigg

Printed by Bayliss Printing Company Ltd of Worksop, UK

Selection © Katharine Towers, 2024

Cover illustration © Caroline Barker, 2024
https://www.carolinebarkerart.co.uk/

Candlestick Press monogram © Barbara Shaw, 2008

© Candlestick Press, 2024

ISBN 978 1 913627 08 9

**Acknowledgements**

The poems in this pamphlet are reprinted from the following books, all by permission of the publishers listed unless stated otherwise. Every effort has been made to trace the copyright holders of the poems published in this book. The editor and publisher apologise if any material has been included without permission, or without the appropriate acknowledgement, and would be glad to be told of anyone who has not been consulted.

Thanks are due to all the copyright holders cited below for their kind permission.

Michael Brown, poem first published in this pamphlet. SL Grange, *bodies, and other haunted houses* (Seren, 2022). Harry Guest, *Puzzling Harvest: Collected Poems 1955-2000* (Anvil Press Poetry, 2002) by permission of Carcanet Press Ltd. Joanna Ingham, *Poetry Wales* (Summer 2020 Volume 56 Number 1) by kind permission of the author. James P Lenfestey, *A Cartload of Scrolls: 100 Poems in the Manner of T'ang Dynasty Poet Han-Shan* (Holy Cow! Press, 2007). Copyright © 2007 by James P Lenfestey. Reprinted with the permission of The Permissions Company, LLC on behalf of Holy Cow! Press, www.holycowpress.org. Kim Moore, poem first appeared on the Ledbury Poetry Festival website by kind permission of the author. Marilyn Nelson, *The Homeplace* (Louisiana State Univ. Press, 1990). Poem copyright ©1990 by Marilyn Nelson. Poem reprinted by permission of Marilyn Nelson and the publisher. Clare Shaw, *Flood* (Bloodaxe Books, 2018) www.bloodaxebooks.com. Anne Stevenson, *Collected Poems* (Bloodaxe Books, 2023) www.bloodaxebooks.com. Claire Walker, *Poetry Wales* (Summer 2021 Volume 57 Number 1) by kind permission of the author.

All permissions cleared courtesy of Dr Suzanne Fairless-Aitken –
Swift Permissions swiftpermissions@gmail.com.

Where poets are no longer living, their dates are given.

# Contents

| | | Page |
|---|---|---|
| Daughter | *James P Lenfestey* | 5 |
| Poem for a Daughter | *Anne Stevenson* | 6 |
| Nancy | *Claire Walker* | 7 |
| Daughter | *SL Grange* | *8 - 9* |
| Teaching Your Daughter to Swim | *Clare Shaw* | 10 |
| For my daughter | *Kim Moore* | *11* |
| Daughters, 1900 | *Marilyn Nelson* | 12 |
| Truce | *Michael Brown* | 13 |
| A Daughter's First Term at University | *Harry Guest* | 14 |
| She tells me she loves me till the last number and what is the last number anyway | *Joanna Ingham* | *15* |

**Daughter**

A daughter is not a passing cloud, but permanent,
holding earth and sky together with her shadow.
She sleeps upstairs like mystery in a story,
blowing leaves down the stairs, then cold air, then warm.
We who at sixty should know everything, know nothing.
We become dull and disoriented by uncertain weather.
We kneel, palms together, before this blossoming altar.

*James P Lenfestey*

## Poem for a Daughter

'I think I'm going to have it,'
I said, joking between pains.
The midwife rolled competent
sleeves over corpulent milky arms.
'Dear, you never have it,
we deliver it.'
A judgement years proved true.
Certainly I've never had you

as you still have me, Caroline.
Why does a mother need a daughter?
Heart's needle, hostage to fortune,
freedom's end. Yet nothing's more perfect
than that bleating, razor-shaped cry
that delivers a mother to her baby.
The bloodcord snaps that held
their sphere together. The child,
tiny and alone, creates the mother.

A woman's life is her own
until it is taken away
by a first particular cry.
Then she is not alone
but part of the premises
of everything there is:
a time, a tribe, a war.
When we belong to the world
we become what we are.


*Anne Stevenson (1933 – 2020)*

**Nancy**

Here is my daughter's favourite toy,
with carved wooden animals carefully placed
in rows of two. She knows them all:
*giraffe, elephant, zebra,* a zoo full

of exotic beasts deemed worth saving.
There are birds on board that she launches
to the sky, seeing only sun on their wings.
Noah is standing at the prow,

figurehead of his floating world,
timber-framed, weather-proof.
On the deck, a wife works:
her anonymous body, her modest tunic.

I imagine this woman, face to the rain,
the nightly voyage of getting creatures fed.
The constant shovelling of shit.
And my daughter, who has not yet

known any storms, plays on, oblivious.
*We should give her a name,* I tell her.
*She deserves her own name.*


*Claire Walker*

## Daughter

Running hard towards the edge of everything
she carried her shoes in her hands
flinging them upwards
to catch on phone lines

Destiny was not a byword for her
the end of the road no kind of border
– patrolled by stray animals and
invitations to roam

Every day began like a shout
a motion into sky
shorts patched and t-shirt grubby
with leaves fallen unnoticed

A cartwheel soul tumbling riot
always mid-air spinning into the river
having leapt the banks
with her heart on her open palms

You are waiting
to hear how she landed broken –
that fate put out a malicious foot
tripped her in the dance

No

Simply, she spins a dandelion
head always, watching
soft white seeds float
downstream with the breeze

Rainbow leggings and a forthright
little mouth ready
to grin and open tender with demands
an O of wonder, an O


*SL Grange*

## Teaching Your Daughter to Swim

in open waters
though you don't know the depth
of the lake at its centre; who might have died there,
whether the pike will scare her or bite her,
if the current will pull her down.

At the level of water, the mountains are higher.
The cold is a world she will walk to and enter
where deep mud is softer than skin.
Let the pebbles swim under her feet.
All the darkness beneath her

is answered by birds
and the trees will be tall and kind.
The sun will light up the water above her.
When there's no ground left to stand on,
then she'll fly.

Though the cold makes her teeth ache
she can take it. The rain cannot soak her,
the swan will not harm her. No dead man
will reach out his hand. You will watch her
leaving the shore behind

and the current will flow
the right way. That day,
the water will hold her
and take her far from you.
Now let her go from you. Let go.

*Clare Shaw*

**For my daughter**

And later, when she asks, I'll say
some parts of it were beautiful –
how in their brightness
and sudden opening
the faces of the neighbours
began to look like flowers.
I'll tell her how we began
to look back at photos
of our younger selves
with our arms around a stranger
or leaning on the shoulders
of friends, and saw that touch
had always been a kind of holiness,
a type of worship we were promised.
I'll tell her that in some ways
our days shrunk to nothing,
being both as long as a year
and as quick as the turning of a page.
I'll tell her how she learned to crawl
in those days, in those times
when we could not leave,
when bodies were carried from homes,
that she began to say her first word
while death waited in the streets,
that though I was afraid,
I never saw fear in her eyes.


*Kim Moore*

**Daughters, 1900**

Five daughters, in the slant light on the porch,
are bickering. The eldest has come home
with new truths she can hardly wait to teach.

She lectures them: the younger daughters search
the sky, elbow each others' ribs, and groan.
Five daughters, in the slant light on the porch

and blue-sprigged dresses, like a stand of birch
saplings whose leaves are going yellow-brown
with new truths. They can hardly wait to teach,

themselves, to be called "Ma'am," to march
high-heeled across the hanging bridge to town.
Five daughters. In the slant light on the porch

Pomp lowers his paper for a while, to watch
the beauties he's begotten with his Ann:
these new truths they can hardly wait to teach.

The eldest sniffs, "A lady doesn't scratch."
The third snorts back, "Knock, knock: nobody home."
The fourth concedes, "Well, maybe not in *church* . . ."
Five daughters in the slant light on the porch.


*Marilyn Nelson*

**Truce**

The late afternoon heat drives us from the house
to the uncomfortable garden bench where we sit
for want of somewhere else.

A truce. I mark time, stare into a world
beyond our makeshift seat. Nothing there
but the intermittent breeze, light air.

We don't speak but when I find a voice
sweltering in my throat, you don't hear
your father's words but something like a distance

being broached. A man calling to his daughter,
a stranger in the closeness and the space,
in the darkness before the evening came.

*Michael Brown*

## A Daughter's First Term at University

You've said good-bye. She's standing in the car-park.
You know there are mallards on that pool in the quadrangle.
A Virginia Creeper sprawls crimson by her balcony.
Later a heron will visit those fields beyond suburbs
but now she has no map to decipher tomorrow,
the clock-face is unyielding, the brochure's out of date, she must
invent a city from scratch and fix names on to strangers.
You know all this. The windscreen-wiper doesn't clear your tears.

Phone-calls with costs reversed will assure you that certain
seminars are fun, friends have been found. The fact remains –
the one whom you loved as an everyday presence has been
elected citizen of a world you'll never inhabit.
She's left, rightly so, to gain where others have given,
she's cut the cord, packed her bags, embarked on adulthood,
leaving a shadowy stair-well humming with memories
up which you'll clamber trying to tune in to the past.

When she returns, the week-day thrown open in welcome
will lead again to the stunted monolith, the marsh with its orchids.
From time to time you'll stand together on the same
light bridge, high-arched, under which the long-legged
ibises strut with ludicrous, delicate care.
You'll watch with pride the way her hands brush dirt off strange
and gleaming ores. You'll be given fragmentary
and garbled accounts of patterns made, unwoven,
forged again in distant centuries and ivory rooms.
You'll pay attention but she's gone so far you'll never quite
catch up that unfamiliar figure on the changing fields.

*Harry Guest (1932 – 2021)*

**She tells me she loves me till the last number and what is the last number anyway**

I tell her I don't know and all the things I don't know
tumble ahead of me into the black hole of her questions.
We look up what comes after trillion, which is as far as I get,
discover quadrillion, quintillion, sextillion
and on to Graham's number, the highest to be used
in a mathematical proof. The last, it seems, is a googolplex:
one followed by a googol zeros. But that is only the last
we have a name for and transfinite numbers are larger
than all finite numbers and may be absolutely infinite.
A single googol is greater than the number of atoms
in the observable universe, which is moving away from us

faster than the speed of light and may be unbounded.
If you wrote out a googolplex the mass of books you'd fill
would be vastly greater than the masses of the Andromeda
and Milky Way galaxies combined. Just writing it would take
many times longer than the accepted age of everything
and out beyond proton decay and the Big Freeze. She is not
intimidated by this. Her body against mine on the sofa
is warm and made of stars. I think about that final zero,
how I will wait for her there with all I can carry.


*Joanna Ingham*